WINTERSLOW PRIMARY SCHOOL
WINTERSLOW

HOW PEOPLE LIVE
LIVING BY THE WATER
JACQUELINE DINEEN

Editorial planning
Jollands Editions

MACMILLAN
EDUCATION

© Macmillan Education Limited 1987
© BLA Publishing Limited 1987

All rights reserved. No reproduction, copy or transmission
of this publication may be made without written permission.

No paragraph of this publication may be reproduced, copied
or transmitted save with written permission or in accordance
with the provisions of the Copyright Act 1956 (as amended),
or under the terms of any licence permitting limited copying
issued by the Copyright Licensing Agency, 33 – 4 Alfred Place,
London WC1E 7DP.

Any person who does any unauthorised act in relation to
this publication may be liable to criminal prosecution and
civil claims for damages.

First published 1987
Reprinted 1987

Published by
MACMILLAN EDUCATION LTD
Houndmills, Basingstoke, Hampshire RG21 2XS
and London
Companies and representatives
throughout the world

Designed and produced by BLA Publishing Limited,
Swan Court, East Grinstead, Sussex, England.

Also in LONDON · HONG KONG · TAIPEI · SINGAPORE · NEW YORK

A Ling Kee Company

Illustrations by Fiona Fordyce and BLA Publishing Limited
Colour origination by Planway Limited
Printed in Hong Kong

British Library Cataloguing in Publication Data

Dineen, Jacqueline
 Living by the water. — (How people live)
 — (Macmillan world library)
 1. Coasts — Juvenile literature
 2. Estuaries — Juvenile literature
 3. Rivers — Juvenile literature
 4. Lakes — Juvenile literature
 I. Title II. Series
 910′.0916   GB451.2

ISBN 0-333-42625-8
ISBN 0-333-42620-7 Series

Acknowledgements
The Publishers wish to thank the following
organizations for their invaluable assistance in the
preparation of this book.

Australian Information Service
Japan National Tourist Organization
RNAS Culdrose
Shell UK Limited

Photographic credits
t = top *b* = bottom *l* = left *r* = right

cover: ZEFA

4 Susan Griggs Agency; 5 Douglas Dickins; 6 Mansell
Collection; 7*t* The Hutchison Library; 7*b* Ivor Edmonds/
Seaphot; 8 ZEFA; 8/9, 9 The Hutchison Library;
10 Chris Fairclough; 11*t*, 11*b*, 12, 13*t* The Hutchison
Library; 13*b* Chris Fairclough; 14/15 The Hutchison
Library; 15*t*, 15*b*, 16 ZEFA; 17 Robert Harding Picture
Library; 18*t* ZEFA; 18*b* John Lythgoe/Seaphot; 19 ZEFA;
20 Chris Fairclough; 21*t* Douglas Dickins; 21*b* ZEFA;
22 The Hutchison Library; 22/23 Barnaby's Picture
Library; 23 Douglas Dickins; 24/25 Ivor Edmonds/
Seaphot; 25 T. & D. Crossley/Seaphot; 26*t* South
American Pictures; 26*b* Japan National Tourist
Organization; 27 J. Allan Cash Photo Library; 28 Susan
Griggs Agency; 29*l* Alex Williams/Seaphot; 29*r* Chris
Fairclough; 30 ZEFA; 31*t* The Hutchison Library;
31*b* Japan National Tourist Organization; 32*t*, 32*b*
Douglas Dickins; 33 ZEFA; 35*t* Mansell Collection;
35*b* Shell UK Limited; 36, 37*t* ZEFA;
37*b* T. & D. Crossley/Seaphot; 38*l*, 38*r* ZEFA; 39 The
Hutchison Library; 40, 41*t*, 41*b* Shell UK Limited;
42 Australian Information Service; 43*t* ZEFA; 43*b* RNAS
Culdrose; 44 The Hutchison Library; 45 Ed Lawrenson

Note to the reader
In this book there are some words in the text which are printed in **bold** type. This shows that the
word is listed in the glossary on page 46. The glossary gives a brief explanation of words which may
be new to you.

Contents

Introduction	4	Life on a trawler	28
Exploring new lands	6	Fishing ports and markets	30
People and rivers	8	Great ports of the past	32
Farming and fishing	10	Trading across oceans	34
Boats and ferries	12	Great ports today	36
Rivers and industry	14	Shipbuilding and repairs	38
Inland ports	16	Life on an oil rig	40
Living by the coast	18	Saving lives	42
Sports and holidays	20	Our need for water	44
The struggle with the sea	22		
Food from the sea	24	Glossary	46
Fishing communities	26	Index	48

Introduction

Nobody can live without water. We all need water to drink, and for washing. Farmers need water to grow crops and for their animals to drink. Some people live by catching and selling fish. Water is used in **factories** and homes. People use water for pleasure. They sail on it and swim in it.

The seas and the oceans cover more than two-thirds of the Earth. This water is **salt water**. We cannot drink salt water because the salt makes us sick. People, plants and animals need **fresh water**. Fresh water comes from rain, rivers, lakes and from under the ground. Only about three per cent of the world's water is fresh water.

Living near water

The first people in the world did not live in one place. They had to move around to look for food and water. Then, about 10 000 years ago, people learned to grow food and keep animals. They needed plenty of water. These first farmers lived near the Tigris and Euphrates Rivers in the Middle East. People began to settle near the coasts, too. They made boats and caught fish from the sea.

Most rain falls near the coast. This means that there is less fresh water in the middle of large areas of land. Australia is a very big land. The centre of Australia is very dry, so few people can live there.

▼ Hong Kong's deep water harbour is one of the busiest in the world. The goods on this ship are being carried in large metal boxes called **containers**.

Introduction

▶ The best way through the forests in Thailand is along the rivers. People live in houses or boats at the edge of the water. They buy fruit and vegetables from the traders who come by boat.

Most people in Australia live near the east coast where it rains the most. Look at a map of the world. You will see that most of the places with large numbers of people, or **populations**, are near lakes, rivers or seas.

Carrying goods by water

The rivers and seas have always been used by people for carrying goods. The people of the past found it easier to move heavy goods by boat than to move them across land. They built villages near the water and travelled by boat to other villages. People began to exchange goods, or to **trade**, with each other. Some villages became centres for trade and grew bigger.

Bigger ships were built as more people traded. People needed safe places to load and unload the ships. Some of the best **harbours** are near the mouths of rivers. There is shelter for the ships and smaller boats can take the goods up the river.

Today, it can be faster to travel by road, rail or air than by water. Even so, many **bulk goods** are carried by sea. It is cheaper to carry large amounts of goods on one ship than to carry many smaller amounts by truck, train or plane.

Exploring new lands

In the past, rivers were often used by people who explored new lands. They found the rivers were the easiest way to travel through unknown country. Rivers make a way through the thick forests where there are no roads. Rivers lead to other rivers, or to the sea.

New lands

About 450 years ago, people from Europe began to explore North and South America. In 1535, the French explorer, Jacques Cartier, travelled up the St Lawrence River in North America. A few years later, the Spanish explorer, Francisco de Orellana, sailed to Peru on the west coast of South America. He crossed the Andes Mountains and found the Amazon River. He travelled down the river and reached its mouth in 1541. For hundreds of years, the river was the only way through the Amazon jungle. Now, there are new roads. They have opened up parts of the forest.

Central Africa was not explored by Europeans until about 150 years ago. In 1855, a Scotsman called David Livingstone crossed Africa from west to east. He followed the Zambezi River to its mouth on the east coast. Henry Stanley travelled along the Congo River (now called the Zaire) in the 1870s. Twenty years later, an English woman called Mary Kingsley went to West Africa to study the life of the African people. She also travelled by river.

These journeys by river helped people to make maps of these lands. Soon, European people began to settle there. Some were farmers. Others came to trade or to set up churches and schools. They took over the land and slowly changed the ways in which the local people lived.

▼ Nearly a hundred years ago, Mary Kingsley travelled along the Ogowe River in West Africa by canoe. This was the best way for her to travel. She met the local people and learned about their way of life.

Exploring new lands

◄ An expedition makes its way through rapids on a river in South America. The journey is slow and hard, but there is no other way through the thick forest.

Shaping a river

People cannot travel by boat along all rivers. Some rivers have waterfalls and **rapids**, where the water flows very fast over rocks. Explorers sometimes had to carry their boats across land to avoid the waterfalls and rapids. Some river mouths break up into lots of small, shallow channels. Only small boats can find a way through.

Today, we can change the shape of rivers. Deep channels can be cut in a shallow river. A machine scoops up, or **dredges**, the mud from the river bed. This makes it safer for ships to use the river. Inland **ports** grow up. There are jobs for people on the river or at the ports. **Locks** can be built beside rapids and waterfalls. A lock raises or lowers ships from one level of water to the next. People dig waterways called **canals** to join one river with another. Canals are also built to straighten out a winding river.

▲ Dredgers are used to make rivers deeper. A dredger digs up the mud from a river bed. The mud is often used to build up the river banks. This stops the river from flooding.

People and rivers

Many of the widest and longest rivers in the world are used for trade. Large ships can sail along these rivers. There is plenty of water for **industry**. The Mississippi in the United States, the Rhine in Europe and the St Lawrence in Canada are three great trade rivers. There are large towns along the banks. Industry makes work for millions of people along these rivers.

The Nile in Egypt and the Ganges in India are great rivers, too. They flow through dry lands. Most of the people who live near these rivers are farmers. They use the water from the rivers to water their crops. Their land would be too dry to grow food without the rivers. Many of the farmers grow just enough food for themselves and their families. People have lived along the Nile and the Ganges for thousands of years. Now, boats bring visitors to see the beautiful buildings of the past. Some local people earn money by selling things to the visitors.

A way of life

Many things happen along a river. Farmers work in the fields and use water from the river. People fish from boats or the river bank. Boats take goods and people up and down the river. Towns and villages are built where there is a harbour for boats or a good place to cross the river. The river is widest near the mouth. Big ships can sail on the river there. The ships can load or unload their goods at a port. A lot of the people work at the port and in the factories nearby.

Some rivers mark the border between one country and the next. The Mekong River divides Thailand and Laos in South

▲ In West Germany, many of the rivers and canals are used for trade. These boats are carrying heavy goods. You can see steel plates on the nearest boat.

People and rivers

East Asia. It is not easy to cross the river. Border guards check the people crossing the bridges. Other rivers, like the Danube in Europe, flow through many countries. **Customs** officers check the boats at the borders.

Riverside villages

In some places, rivers are still the best way to carry goods and people a long way. Boats bring trade to the people who live beside the river. The Ijaw people live near the mouth of the Niger River in West Africa. The river floods often and the land is too marshy for farming. The people live in houses built on **stilts**. The stilts raise the houses above the level of the river. The Ijaws live by fishing. They catch fish in the river and in the sea. Then, they take the fish by boat to the villages further up the river. They sell the fish so that they can buy yams, bananas and rice.

▲ There is plenty of river traffic on the Zaire River in Africa. The local people try to sell goods to the large boats which move up and down the river.

◀ The level of a river rises after heavy rainfall. Some rivers rise and fall by several metres each year. These riverside houses in Papua New Guinea are built on stilts. This protects them from floods.

Farming and fishing

▼ In South East Asia, the main crop is rice. Rice needs plenty of water to grow. Water is carried along irrigation channels from the rivers to the fields.

Rivers help to provide food. People can eat the fish they catch in the river, or sell the fish to other people. The soil beside a river is often very good for growing crops in.

As a river nears the sea, it flows over flatter land. After heavy rain, the river floods. The flat land beside the river is called a **flood plain**. The flood leaves behind a layer of rich, **fertile** soil.

Rivers carry sand and mud, or **silt**, into the sea. If the sea does not wash the silt away, the silt divides the river into small channels at its mouth. The channels and the land in between them are called **deltas**. Delta land, like the mouths of the Nile in Egypt and the Ganges in India, is very fertile. People farm the land but it can be dangerous because deltas flood often.

Water for the crops

In a dry land, the farmers have to find ways of carrying water to their crops. This is called **irrigation**. The people of Egypt **invented** ways to do this thousands of years ago. One way is to use a **shaduf**. A shaduf works like a see-saw. There is a long pole with a bucket at one end and a heavy weight at the other. The shaduf is used to lift water from a river. People still use this method today.

Other newer methods of irrigation have made farming easier. Huge barriers, or **dams**, have been built across many rivers. A dam stops the flow of a river. A lake forms behind the dam. The water from the lake flows down pipes to the farmland. The Aswan dam was built on the Nile in 1965. The river does not flood any more. The

Farming and fishing

farmers have water all the year round, but the soil is not so rich.

The large lake, or **reservoir**, that forms behind a dam often takes the land from the local people. Fishermen and farmers from six villages in Hong Kong had to move to flats in a new town. The reservoirs made by new dams covered their homes and farmland.

River fishing

In some countries, people have a choice of many types of food. In other places, there is very little to eat except fish from the local river.

The Kokoto people fish on the Logone and Chari Rivers near Lake Chad in Africa. They fish in two groups. One group of fishermen block the river at night with their boats and spread their nets. The other group make the fish swim towards the nets by beating the water with their paddles.

▲ The *sakia* is a very old way of moving water from one channel to a higher one. The people of Egypt used this and other methods thousands of years ago.

▼ These people are fishing in the Zaire River in Africa. They hang baskets from the frame in the background. The baskets trap the fish.

Boats and ferries

Thousands of years ago, people used logs to travel by water. They sat on a log and floated down a river. Logs tied together make rafts. Whole families could travel on a raft. Then, people learned to make **dugout** canoes. The inside of a log is hollowed out to make a simple boat. Some people on the islands of the Pacific still make dugout canoes.

People began to build better boats. They made wooden paddles, which helped them to move through the water. Then, they learned to use sails. When the wind blew on the sails, the boats moved along.

On rivers today, there are sailing boats, rowing boats and boats with engines. Some of the boats are used for pleasure and others are working boats. On shallow rivers, the boats have flat bottoms so that they will not stick in the mud. On some rivers like the Ganges in India, people use poles to push their small boats through the water. The pole touches the river bed and the boatman pushes the boat forward.

The load carriers

Some boats are made to carry heavy loads. A **barge** is a river boat which has plenty of space for heavy goods, like grain. Barges are long but narrow so they can pass through locks. They have shallow **draughts** so they do not need deep water. On the Mississippi, rows of barges carry grain, oil, coal and iron down the river to the port of New Orleans. Barges also travel along the Rhine. They take cargoes from Switzerland, France and Germany to the port of Rotterdam in the Netherlands. Barge crews spend their lives moving from place to place. Some barges have enough room for families to live on them. The barge is their home.

▼ The Ganges in India is a very crowded river. Boats carry people and goods to the towns along the banks. Most of the river is shallow, so the boats have flat bottoms.

Boats and ferries

Ferry boats carry people and goods from one side of a river to the other. Some people use them every day to go to work or to the shops. Large ferry boats can take cars, buses and trucks. Some ferries are only small rowing boats, or boats pulled across the river by a rope.

Pleasure boats

Rivers are not only used for trade. Many rivers have become places for fun and sport. Some people row, sail or canoe on the rivers at weekends and holidays. Other people travel along the rivers in pleasure cruisers. These are motor boats with a cabin to sleep in. Once the River Thames in England had **warehouses** and industries along its banks. Now, in the summer, it is crowded with pleasure boats. At places like Marlow and Windsor, tourists can leave their boats and have a meal or buy food and other goods.

▲ Not all boats are used for transport. Some people live in floating homes called houseboats. This is a houseboat in Kashmir, India.

▼ Narrowboats and barges once carried goods on Britain's canals. The boats had to be narrow to pass through the narrow locks. Today, many of these canal boats are used for holidays.

13

Rivers and industry

Industry needs power and transport. Rivers offer both. In the past, people used river power to turn **waterwheels**. The wheels turned machines like grinders and hammers. Farmers took their wheat to watermills where it was made into flour. Some of these mills still work today.

A lot of water is used in making things like steel, clothes and food. Factories are often on river banks. Houses are built nearby for the people who work in the factories. Towns and cities grow up as more people come to work in shops, schools, hospitals and hotels.

Sometimes a factory cannot sell its **products**. It has to make fewer goods. It may even have to shut down. People lose their jobs. If there are no other jobs in the area, people may have to move away to find work. The whole town suffers if the factories close.

From logs to paper

The paper making industry uses large amounts of water. Paper mills are often by rivers. Most paper is made from trees. One way to bring logs to a paper mill is to float them down a river. In the past, this was the easiest way. Not all forests, though, are near rivers. Today, truck drivers bring most of the logs by road. Paper mills provide many different jobs. At the mill, the logs are chopped into tiny pieces and mixed with water. This makes a wet mixture called **pulp**. Pulp is also made by soaking the wood in chemicals. The pulp is put on to a paper making machine. Most of the water drains out of the pulp and leaves a wide band of paper. The paper is pressed into a sheet between huge rollers.

▲ Thousands of floating logs wait to be cut up at a sawmill in Finland. The logs have been towed through rivers and lakes to reach the mill. This is a cheap and easy way of transporting the logs from the forest.

Power stations

The first industries used water power to work their machines. Now, most factories use **electricity**. Water is still important. Electricity is made at **power stations**. A power station has large machines, called **turbines**, which turn very fast to make the electricity. The turbines are turned by jets of steam. The steam is made by heating water in large boilers. Large amounts of water are needed, so many power stations are built near rivers.

Rivers and industry

▲ Large amounts of water are needed to make paper. The water is mixed with the wood chips to make a pulp. The pulp is pressed and dried as it passes through huge machines. Some machines can produce 30 km of paper in one hour.

◀ Power stations use so much water that they are often built near rivers. This one in West Germany supplies electricity to people living in the nearby city of Cologne.

Rushing water can also turn turbines to make electricity. The water must flow very fast to turn the turbines. Even a fast-flowing river is not fast enough. A dam has to be built across a river. A large dam may take years to build. Hundreds of people are needed for the work. A large lake builds up behind the dam. When gates in the dam are opened, water surges through a tunnel. The water strikes the turbines in the tunnel with great power. The movement of the turbines makes electricity. Electricity made with water power is called **hydro-electricity**.

Inland ports

Most ports are built near the mouths of rivers or on the coasts. The water there is deep enough for large ships. Some ports are far away from the sea. They are built on wide, deep rivers, or on the edge of lakes. Large ships can sail inland and unload their cargoes.

Ports are important to a country's **economy**. Very few countries can provide all the things which the people need. They have to buy, or **import**, goods from other countries. To pay for these goods, they sell, or **export**, goods abroad. Many of the goods are carried by water.

Great cities have grown up around inland ports. Paris in France stands on the Seine and Marne Rivers. Paris is nearly 200 km from the sea but barges can reach it. Chicago is one of the ports on the Great Lakes in North America. Ships travel from the lakes to the Atlantic Ocean along the St Lawrence Seaway.

◀ Chicago's position on Lake Michigan has helped to make it a large industrial city. A canal links the city with the Illinois and Mississippi Rivers.

Inland ports

▲ Port Harcourt provides jobs for people who prefer to work in the city. Some work at the docks and others work in industries nearby.

St Louis

Today, the city of St Louis is a large inland port on the Mississippi River in North America. Before 1800, St Louis was a small settlement of fur traders. Most people in North America lived near the east coast. Then, more people came to North America. There was not enough work for all of them. They began to move west in search of new farmland. At St Louis, they crossed the wide river dividing the country into east and west. St Louis became known as the 'gateway to the west'.

The Mississippi is the longest river in the United States. It is part of the world's largest inland waterway system. St Louis lies halfway between the Great Lakes and New Orleans. The city is a market for grain, wool, farm animals and wood. Goods arrive by rail and road too, but river transport is cheaper. Many people live and work in St Louis. They work in factories, offices, or at the port.

Port Harcourt

Port Harcourt is the second largest port in Nigeria in Africa. It lies 66 km inland on the Bonny River. The port was built in 1912. Coal, tin and palm oil were brought to Port Harcourt by river and rail. Ships then took the goods to other countries.

Oil was found in Nigeria in 1956. Soon, oil **tankers** were using Port Harcourt. Since the 1960s, new **docks** and oil **refineries** have been built at Port Harcourt. People came from the villages to work in the new oil industries.

In recent years, the price of oil has dropped. The Nigerians buy fewer goods now from other countries. More farmers are needed but people do not want to go back to the villages. The schools and houses are better in the towns.

17

Living by the coast

Some people make their living by the sea. They may be fishermen or work in the tourist industry. Some people go to live by the sea when they retire from work. The sea air is fresh and healthy. Life in many seaside towns is quieter than in big cities.

Many towns along the coasts are tourist **resorts**. People come to stay for their holidays because the towns are attractive. Some seaside towns have no other types of industry. The towns and villages are crowded in the summer and empty in the winter each year. There is less work in the winter months.

▲ Majorca is a Spanish island in the Mediterranean Sea. The island's main industry is tourism. Visitors come from all over northern Europe to enjoy the sun and the beaches.

◀ This man is raking salt into piles. Sea salt is collected mainly in the warm parts of the world. The hot sun is needed to dry out the sea water.

Living by the coast

Gifts from the sea

The sea supplies us with more than food. There are other **resources** in the sea. In some countries, people collect the salt from sea water. They make pools of sea water which dry out in the sun. The salt is left behind. Salt is added to most food made in factories.

Coral and pearls come from the sea. They are made into jewellery. Coral comes from tiny sea animals which live in the warm waters of the world. Pearls come from the pearl oyster. Pearl oysters are not the same as the oysters which people eat. Pearl oysters live in warm seas. A pearl is made if a grain of sand gets inside an oyster shell. The oyster surrounds the grain of sand with layers of pearl to protect itself. Pearl divers hold their breath and dive into the sea to find the oysters. Divers collect sponges from the sea bed too. Real bath sponges cost a lot of money.

Up and down the coast

Traders still carry some goods in small ships from one port to another along the coast. Heavy things like sand and coal can be carried more cheaply by ship. The industries that use them are often by the sea.

The Arab people have traded along the coasts of the Indian Ocean for hundreds of years. Long ago, they learned to find their way south by using the stars. The Arabs sailed their boats, called **dhows**, all the way down the east coast of Africa. They were blown along by the strong **monsoon** winds. The Arabs set up trading posts in places like Zanzibar and Madagascar. Arab dhows still call at these ports.

▶ An Arab dhow sails down the east coast of Africa. The sail of the dhow can be moved to catch the wind. This allows the dhow to sail in any direction.

Sports and holidays

▼ Water sports can be fun even for beginners. The basic skills have to be learned first. Some people join clubs so they can learn the skills and race in teams.

Many people go to the coast for a holiday. Some people like to lie on the beach. Other people enjoy a more active holiday. They swim or go out in boats. Some coasts have big waves. People like to ride, or surf, on these waves. A surfer lies or stands on a long, narrow board. Windsurfing is another water sport. The windsurfer stands on a board called a sailboard. The wind blows against the sail and carries the board through the water.

Many seaside towns depend on the tourist trade. Tourists come to enjoy themselves. They spend money in the towns. Many of the people who live there work in hotels, cafés or gift shops. People come to the seaside towns to find jobs. Everyone works very hard all through the summer.

Water sports

Seaside resorts with a good harbour are full of people and boats at holiday time. Sailing boats vary in size. Some are only two or three metres long. They can be sailed by one or two people. The ocean-going racing yachts need a bigger **crew**. These boats have cabins where people can sleep. They also have engines in case there is no wind.

Some people enjoy the thrill of power-boat racing. Power-boats have

Sports and holidays

engines and some go very fast. These boats can pull waterskiers along behind them. The waterskiers wear two flat skis and hold on to a rope attached to the back of a boat. Waterskiing is popular in places where the sea is warm.

The winter months

Many seaside towns are very quiet in the winter. Sometimes the hotels close down. People move away to find work. Whole villages close down in parts of Greece. The people move inland to farm or go back to the cities.

Most people have their longest holiday in the summer. If they go to the sea, they want sunshine. Tropical islands, like Barbados in the Caribbean Sea or the Seychelles in the Indian Ocean, have tourists all the year round. It is always hot and sunny.

▲ La Grande Motte is a tourist resort in France. All the holiday apartments, hotels, shops, restaurants and the harbour for boats were built just for the tourists.

▼ Seaside resorts are often empty in the winter. Many hotels, restaurants and shops close. The hotels which stay open offer lower prices.

The struggle with the sea

The land near the coast is always under attack from the sea. The sea beats against the beaches and the cliffs. In windy weather, huge waves crash on to the shore. The sea slowly wears away the land. This is called **erosion**. People have built strong sea walls along the bottom of some cliffs. These protect the cliffs from erosion. Sometimes, houses are built near the edge of a cliff. Without the wall, the cliff will crumble and the buildings will fall into the sea.

Some land near the coast is very low and flat. The seas and rivers often flood this land. It is difficult for people to live there. They have to build walls and drain the land to stop the flooding.

Taking land from the sea

In some countries, people have taken land from the sea. The Netherlands is a very flat country. Much of the land lies below sea level. The Dutch people have built earth walls called **dikes**. The dikes hold back the sea and stop the rivers from flooding. About 500 years ago, the people began to drain the watery land. They needed new farmland and land for houses. Windmills were built to pump the water from the land into canals and ditches. Then people grew **reeds**. The reeds helped to bind the mud together and to make soil. A piece of land that is saved in this way is called a **polder**. The Dutch polders are very rich farmland.

The Netherlands have to keep up the struggle with the sea. Today, pumping stations keep water off the land.

◄ The sea used to cover this part of the Netherlands. The windmills were built to help drain the land. The wind turned the sails of the windmills to work water pumps. They pumped the water away from the low-lying land.

The struggle with the sea

Homes on the water

In some countries, people make their homes on boats. There are floating villages in parts of South America, Africa and South East Asia.

Hong Kong Island is one of the most crowded islands in the world. Each year some new land is made by filling bits of the sea with rubbish. It is enough to build a new road or perhaps an industrial estate. Most people live in tall, crowded buildings. Some people live on the water in large sailing boats called junks. These people used to earn their living by fishing or by carrying cargo. Now, many of them work on land. They use their boats as places to live.

▼ Many Chinese families live on boats around Hong Kong. The boats are grouped together in 'floating villages'. This family lives next to a floating restaurant. The decorations are for the Chinese New Year.

▲ The sea is eroding the soft cliffs. Part of the garden wall has already fallen down the cliff.

Food from the sea

About 75 million tonnes of fish are caught each year. Some countries have large fishing fleets which go to sea for months at a time. They store the fish they catch in freezers. This keeps the fish fresh until the boat gets back to port. This type of fishing is called deep-sea fishing.

In other places, fishing has not changed much for hundreds of years. The fishermen go out in small boats and catch the fish with nets, lines and traps. They stay out on the water only for a day. The fish they bring back is fresh. This type of fishing is called inshore fishing.

▼ **This boat is returning from a day's fishing off the coast of Gambia, West Africa. A crowd of people from the fishing village help to pull the heavy boat up the beach.**

Inshore fishing

In a fishing village by the coast, almost everyone has a job to do with fishing. Many of the people are fishermen. Old people repair the nets. There are shops selling fishing equipment. Some people build and repair the boats. Restaurants cook the fresh fish.

Some inshore fishing boats are 25 m long. Many are much smaller than this. The fishermen use nets or long lines. A long line is a long rope which has small lines branching from it. Each line has a hook and bait on the end.

The crew find the fish with the help of an echo sounder. This is a machine which sends out sound waves under the water. The sound waves bounce back to the boat when they touch a large group, or **shoal**, of fish. This tells the crew where the fish are.

Fishermen must be careful not to **over-fish** an area. If they catch too many fish from one area, there will be no new fish to catch later on.

Food from the sea

▲ These fishermen are laying lobster pots off the coast of Ireland. They leave markers to tell them where the pots are. They will return the next day to pick up the catch.

Shellfish

Shellfish are sea animals with hard shells. Most of them live on the sea bed. Many people like to eat them. About 2.5 million tonnes are caught each year. There are several ways of catching shellfish. Lobsters and crabs are caught in small traps called pots. The fishermen put some bait in the pots and leave them on the sea bed.

Shrimps and prawns are caught in a **trawl** net. A boat drags the trawl net along the sea bed. It scoops up the fish in its path. Octopus and squid are also caught in trawl nets.

Mussels attach themselves to rocks and can be picked off by hand. Oysters live on the sea bed. They are scooped up by a special type of net which has a steel frame. The net is towed by a fishing boat. Fish farmers breed oysters in oyster 'beds' near the shore. Millions of tiny oysters are sent each year from an English oyster farm to Spain and Italy. They grow more quickly in the warmer water. They are ready to eat in two years.

# Fishing communities

Some countries depend on fishing to feed their people. They have large fleets of deep-sea boats. Fishing also helps their economy because they sell fish to other countries. Japan, China and the USSR catch the most fish.

Many types of fish can be bought at shops and markets around the world. Some fish, like cod, like very cold water. Others, like tuna, prefer warmer seas. Some fish, like herring, swim near the surface. Others, like plaice, live near the sea bed. Fishermen have to know where each type of fish lives. The deep-sea fleets go all over the world in search of fish. Before the days of freezers, people ate the types of fish from the sea nearby. Today, people can enjoy many more types.

▲ A large fishing boat may catch 50 tonnes of fish in one haul. This catch of anchovies is being sucked aboard the boat through a pipe.

◀ Fish markets in Japan sell all types of fish. The Japanese eat the fish in many different ways. They like it raw, dried, smoked, steamed or pickled.

Fishing communities

► Fish drying on racks in Iceland. Drying and smoking are two ways of keeping fish for a long time. Today, most fish is kept by freezing it.

Japan's fishing industry

More than 100 million people live in Japan. The country has many mountains and there is not much farmland. People rely on food from the sea. About one-fifth of the people work in the fishing industry. Some of these people are inshore fishermen. They catch many types of fish like cod, herring, sardines, sharks and squid.

Japan has to guard against over-fishing near her coast. The inshore fishermen cannot catch enough fish for everyone. Deep-sea fleets fish in the Atlantic and Pacific Oceans. They like to catch tuna. Japan sells tuna all over the world.

Shellfish sell well in Japan. There are fish farms where shellfish are grown. The Japanese have tried to increase the numbers of shellfish near their shores. They lower tanks with open sides down to the sea bed. The shellfish lay their eggs in these tanks. People can make sure that the eggs hatch out safely.

A long history

Iceland has a very small population compared with Japan. Only 220 000 people live there. Iceland is an island just south of the Arctic Circle. The climate is not good for farming and the island is a long way from other countries.

Iceland's main industry is fishing. Large numbers of herring and mackerel live in the sea near Iceland. The fishermen of Japan catch fish to feed the Japanese people. Most fishermen in Iceland catch most of their fish to sell to other countries. Nearly all of Iceland's exports are fish. Iceland has sold fish to other countries for hundreds of years. New ways of fishing and storing the fish have helped the people of Iceland to build a larger fishing industry. They earn money to pay for comfortable homes and to build good schools, hospitals and roads. Without fish, the people would struggle to survive. They will only let their boats fish in the waters around Iceland.

Life on a trawler

▼ This boat is fishing for halibut off the coast of North America. Halibut is a flat fish which lives near the sea bed. It is caught by using a long line or by trawling.

Deep-sea fishermen go out to sea in boats called **trawlers**. These boats have big trawl nets. The largest type of trawler is a stern trawler. Some of these boats are 70 m long and have crews of 80 people. Stern trawlers have nets which are towed along behind the boat. The catch is pulled in over the back, or stern, of the boat. The stern trawlers are like floating factories.

In many countries the fishermen use smaller boats called side trawlers. These boats are about 25 m long. The net of a side trawler is let out and hauled in over the side of the boat. These boats leave ports around Britain, Spain and Iceland for the rough waters of the North Sea. They hope to catch plenty of cod, haddock, whiting, sole and plaice.

The crew

A side trawler has a crew of seven. The skipper is in charge. He steers the boat and finds the fish. The skipper has equipment to help him. The boat has **navigation instruments**, an echo sounder and a radio to contact other boats.

The engineer keeps the engine running smoothly. The cook makes sure everyone is well fed. The rest of the crew are deckhands. They help with the net. When

Life on a trawler

the skipper finds large shoals of fish, the net is put into the water. The boat drags the net along for about four hours. When the net is hauled in, it is full of fish. After a catch, the deckhands repair the nets and clean the decks. The crew work on deck most of the time. Life on a deep-sea trawler can be cold and wet.

Below decks

Every time a catch is hauled in, the crew **gut** the fish. They remove the insides of each fish so that it will not rot. Then the crew pack the fish in boxes of ice below decks. The ice keeps the fish fresh until the boat gets back to port.

The big stern trawlers have very comfortable living quarters, but there is not much space on a small trawler. The skipper has his own cabin, and there is another cabin where the crew sleep.

The boat stays at sea for about a week. The crew work day and night. They get very tired. At last it is time to go home. They will have a few days' rest before the next trip.

▼ The wheelhouse of a trawler is full of equipment. The skipper can contact the shore and other boats by radio. He has instruments to help him find his way.

▼ A catch is hauled aboard a side trawler in the North Sea. When the net is opened, the fish tumble out on to the deck. They will be stored in boxes below decks.

29

Fishing ports and markets

The fishing fleet returns to its home port when the boats are full of fish. If the weather is bad, they may have to go home without a catch. At the port, people wait to welcome the fleet. The port is noisy and busy. The **quays** are crowded with people.

At last, the boats sail into the harbour and tie up at the quay. The families worry when the fleet is at sea. They know it is a dangerous life and they are happy when the boats get home safely. The families live on the money the fishermen make from selling the catch.

The buyers wait to see what the catch is like. They want to look at it as soon as it is unloaded. They will buy the fish for the markets and **fishmongers** in the towns and the cities.

▶ A fisherman sells his catch on a beach in Oman. Local people will come to buy the fish direct from the fisherman.

◀ These fishermen in Thailand are unloading their catch. They pack the baskets of fish with ice to keep the fish fresh.

Fishing ports and markets

Unloading the catch

The crew's work is not over until the catch is unloaded. Fish that is not frozen is called 'wet' fish. It must be unloaded quickly. The fish can only be sold while it is fresh. In the big ports, the boats come in early in the morning. People called porters help to unload the boxes of fish. The big ports have indoor fish markets where the buyers can look at the fish before they decide what to buy. The fish is sorted into types and sizes and laid out in boxes.

Selling the fish

In a small port, the inshore fishermen often sell their fish on the quayside. Local people come to buy it. They want fish fresh from the boat.

The fishermen hope to get a good **market price** for their fish. The market price depends on the demand. Sometimes, there is a shortage of fish. The buyers want more fish than they can have. This makes the price go up. If too many fish are caught, the price goes down.

At the large ports, the fish is sold by **auction**. When the buyers have looked at the fish, the fish seller calls out a low price for each box of fish. The price goes up if more than one buyer wants to buy a box. The buyer who offers the most money gets the fish. A Dutch auction works the other way round. The seller starts with a high price. He brings the price down until he finds a buyer.

The fish leaves the port in freezer trucks. It is taken to towns and cities all over the country. Some of the fish goes to factories, where it is made into products like fish fingers or animal food. Fish is also frozen or tinned for export.

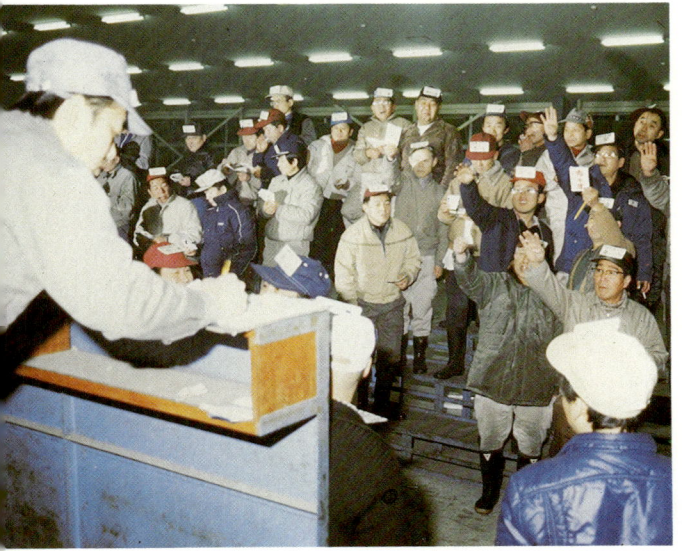

◄ Fish markets are crowded, noisy places. The fish seller's job is to sell the fish for as high a price as possible. In the end, just one buyer will agree to pay a higher price than all the others.

Great ports of the past

There are many ancient ports around the Mediterranean Sea. About 4000 years ago, the people of Egypt started to make wooden sailing ships. They began to trade with other countries along the Mediterranean coast. Later, the Greeks and Romans built larger ships from tall trees. They sailed their ships all over the Mediterranean. They carried grain, wine and valuable goods like gold and **ivory**.

Venice

Venice is a city built on small islands off the coast of Italy. The first people to live there were fishermen. They sold fish and salt to villages on the mainland. People came to the islands to escape wars in Italy. They built ships and traded with other people around the coasts. They were good sailors and fighters. Ships from Venice controlled all the **routes** on the Mediterranean. **Merchants** and skilled craftworkers came to Venice. They built fine houses and travelled through the canals of the city on long, narrow boats called gondolas.

▲ Amsterdam's canals were dug nearly 400 years ago. The canals were used mainly to carry goods. Today the canals are a good way for visitors to see the city.

▶ The canals of Venice are the main routeways through the city. People used to travel by gondola until the motor boat was invented. There are still gondolas in Venice. Tourists pay to ride in them.

Great ports of the past

In 1498, the Portuguese explorer, Vasco da Gama, found a new trade route to the East by sailing around Africa. Now ships could sail all the way from ports like London and Amsterdam to India and China. The trade in silks, **spices** and gold moved to northern Europe. Ships stopped using the Mediterranean route to the East. Fewer ships came to Venice.

Now some people in Venice work in the new harbour or the oil refinery. It is still a trading port but tourism earns more money for the city.

The need for change

Boston is one of the oldest cities in the United States. It was founded on the Charles River by English settlers in 1630. The area around Boston was called New England. Soon, Boston was the main port for ships sailing to England and the West Indies.

By the 1700s, Boston was a large centre for building ships and for fishing. Rich merchants had moved into the city. They sold fish, rum and salt to other ports. Ships brought silk and tea from China, sugar from the West Indies and gold from Africa. New England became America's first industrial region. Factories made cloth from cotton and silk, and leather goods.

More people came to America. Towns were built in the south, where cotton grows. Factories there made cloth more cheaply than in Boston. Many factories in Boston closed. The port was less busy, too. People and goods began to travel by train and by plane. Boston needed new jobs. It became a centre of learning, business and art. There is a new **container** port and computer industries.

▼ Boston, in the United States, is a busy port. Large container ships carry iron, steel, paper and sugar to and from the docks. The old parts of the port are now used for pleasure boats. Trees have been planted. It is a place for people to walk and relax.

Trading across oceans

About 500 years ago, explorers set out across the great oceans of the world. These explorers brought home stories of new lands and the people who lived there. Some explorers went in search of new trade routes.

People were always looking for new routes for their ships and for new trade markets. Christopher Columbus tried to find a new route from Europe to China and India. He sailed west across the Atlantic Ocean and came to America in 1492. Ferdinand Magellan found a way around the world in 1520.

Trade with the East

The Portuguese were the first to find the trade routes around Africa and India. These made journeys from Europe easier and cheaper. Groups of merchants started new trading companies. The most famous ones were the English East India Company and the Dutch East India Company. Ships left Europe for India, China and the East Indies. They carried lead, copper, wines and other goods made in Europe. The ships came back with silks, spices, china and furniture. By 1670, the East India companies were also trading with Japan. The sailors timed their journeys to catch the winds which blew at certain times of the year. The winds were named the trade winds.

People from Europe went to live in other parts of the world. About 150 years ago, fast sailing ships called **clippers** took people to Australia and America to find gold. The clippers brought wool back from Australia. They carried tea from China to America and England. Tea sold for high prices so only rich people could afford to drink it.

▼ The map shows the routes of the sea voyages made by Christopher Columbus, Vasco da Gama and Ferdinand Magellen. Their sea voyages and many others helped world trade to begin.

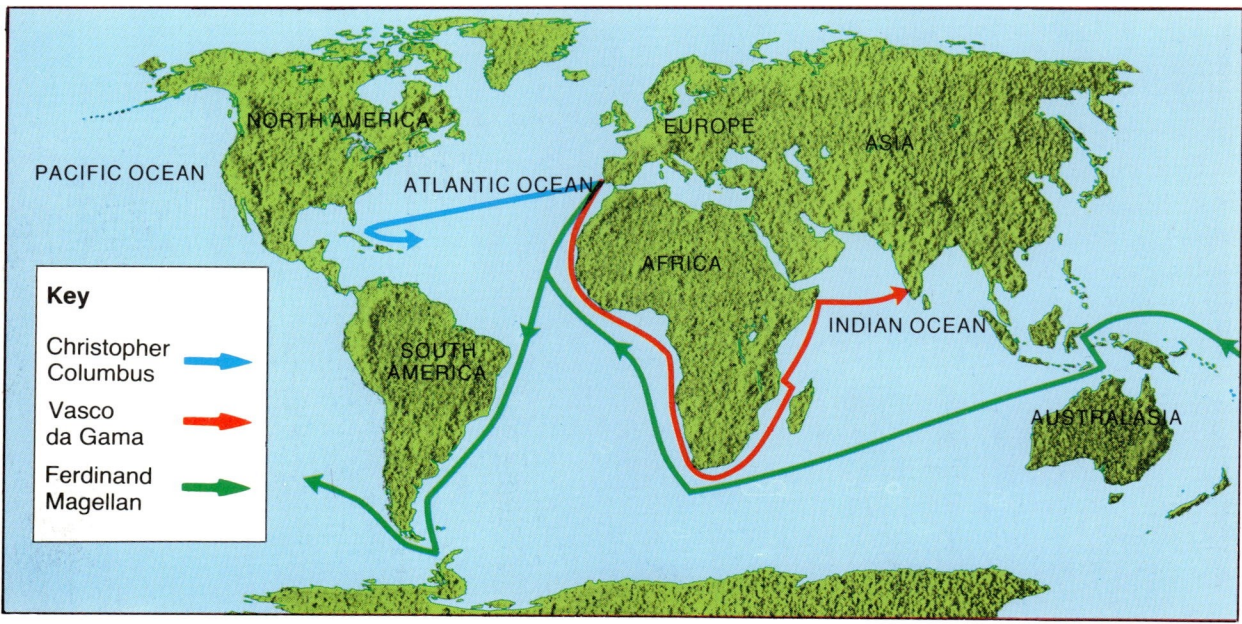

Trading across oceans

▲ In the 1600s, the people of Europe were eager to build up trade with the Far East. This old picture shows gifts being brought from the Dutch people.

A life at sea

Life at sea was dangerous in the days of the sailing ships. Storms wrecked many ships. There was also the danger of attack by pirates. Life below decks was cramped. On a long voyage, food could not be kept fresh. The sailors became ill because they ate bad food.

Today, ships are bigger and safer. Some ships are so large they have shops and hospitals. The crew can watch films in their spare time.

One of the most valuable cargoes today is **crude oil**. Crude oil is the name for oil when it comes out of the ground. It is sold and made into other products like petrol. Giant ships called Very Large Crude Carriers (VLCC) carry crude oil from countries with oil wells to those without oil wells. The cost of carrying the oil is cheaper on a very large ship. Huge tankers travel around Africa from the Middle East to Europe. They do not stop at any ports on the way. Some oil carriers are too big to use most ports. They unload the oil at sea into pipes which bring the oil to the land.

▼ The biggest ships in the world are called Very Large Crude Carriers (VLCC). Their crews' quarters are comfortable. Some crew members travel with their wives. They are at sea for weeks at a time.

Great ports today

The world's busiest ports are in the countries which sell the most goods. Some of the busiest ports include New York in the United States, Rotterdam in Europe and Yokohama in Japan.

A large port has many parts. There are docks with tall cranes. The cranes are used to load and unload the ships. The cargoes are checked at the **terminals**. There are special buildings to store grain and cold stores for food. There are **dry docks**, where ships are repaired and painted. The passengers for cruise ships and ferries check in at special terminals. There is a railway station for the passengers who arrive by train. Cars and trucks drive on to the ferries.

Loading and unloading

A big port handles all types of cargo. Some ships are built to carry grain. The loose grain is poured into the ships through pipes. Other ships are built to carry liquids like oil. The oil is pumped into the ships from huge storage tanks on shore. It takes a long time to load and unload smaller items. Many types of cargo are carried in containers. Some containers are packed at the factories where the goods are made. These containers are carried by road or rail to the port. Other cargoes are packed into containers at the port. The containers are all the same size and shape. A crane loads the containers on to a container ship. This is a fast and cheap way of loading. Container ports do not have to employ many workers because much of the work is done by machines. Dock workers have to find other jobs. Sometimes, new businesses start near the port. People build offices and factories where there is good transport.

◀ This is the busy port of Rotterdam. Some of the ships are unloading their cargoes into barges. The barges will take the cargoes by river to inland ports in northern Europe.

Great ports today

▲ Large ships are towed out to sea by tugs. These small boats have very powerful engines.

▼ A pilot climbs on board a ship before it reaches port. The pilot will join the captain on the bridge of the ship and guide it into the harbour.

People in a port

There are many different jobs in a port. First, the ships have to get to the docks. A **pilot** meets the ships coming into the port and guides them in safely. A large ship is often helped by small boats called tugs. A rope joins the tugboat to the ship. The ship may have to go through a lock to enter the dock. The tugboat crew turns the ship so that it can get to the quay. Dock workers unload the cargoes.

The harbour master is in charge of the port, and the port has its own harbour police. All cargoes and passengers have to pass through customs. The customs officers make sure that people pay taxes on imported goods. The customs officers also check that people are not carrying forbidden goods, such as guns and drugs.

Many other people work in the terminal offices. Visitors and business people need restaurants, banks and hotels, too.

Shipbuilding and repairs

The first boat builders made their boats out of bundles of reeds tied together. These plants grew in the rivers and were easy to cut. People still use these boats on the Tigris and Euphrates Rivers in the Middle East.

Wood is stronger than reeds and it floats well in water. People learned to carve wood and join pieces together. They made bigger boats. At first they rowed their boats with wooden oars. Then, people found that the wind helped to move their boats through the water. They attached sails to the boats.

People have used the basic ideas, or plans, of the first boat builders for thousands of years. The **design** of the Arab dhow has not changed for centuries. The **hull** is made from planks of wood on a frame of wooden ribs. Whole families help to build a new boat and make the sails.

▲ This giant ship is being built on a slipway in the Italian port of Ancona. Hundreds of people take part in building the ship. Many of the parts are made in other countries. The people who made them may never see the finished ship.

◀ These people are building an Arab dhow. The frame of the hull is made of curved wooden ribs. The ribs are attached to planks on the outside. The finished dhow will be very strong.

Shipbuilding and repairs

Building a giant

Today, large ships are made of steel. Hundreds of people take part in building a ship. First, the designers draw the plans. They use computers to help with the design. Small models of the boats are built to check and test the design.

The hull of the ship is made of large steel plates which are attached to a steel frame. Some ships are built on **slipways**. A slipway is a slope which runs down to a river or harbour. The ship slides down the slipway when it is built. Other ships are built in dry docks. Water is let into the dry dock when the ship is finished.

After the launch, the ship is towed to a quay for **fitting out**. The engines are put in. Workmen build the cabins and cargo holds. The ship is fitted with navigation aids, computers and other equipment.

Repairs

A new ship costs a lot to build. Shipping companies use their ships for many years. Only Japan and Korea have large shipbuilding industries today. The demand for new ships is low. Many people who used to work in shipyards have had to find other work.

All ships have to be repaired from time to time. They have to be checked for strength and repainted. The worn-out parts have to be replaced. Some ships are **refitted** to bring them up to date. Most countries have repair yards and dry docks where this work is done.

▼ In some places, the shipyards have closed because demand for new ships is so low. The workers have had to find other jobs and the buildings along the waterfronts are now empty.

39

Life on an oil rig

People first drilled for oil about a hundred years ago. Most of the oil came from under the land. Today, more and more oil comes from under the sea.

How do people find oil under the sea? People called **geologists** study rocks. They know that some types of rock contain oil. They make tests, or **surveys**, from ships. Their instruments tell them about the layers of rock under the sea bed. The geologists tell the oil workers where to drill. They have to drill into the rock to find the oil. The geologists do not always choose the right place! An **exploration rig** is taken to the site. Divers set up the legs on the sea bed. The drilling pipes are in the **derrick**. This is a tall tower on top of the rig.

An exploration rig can be towed from place to place. About 70 people work on a rig. They include the drilling team, divers, engineers and geologists. If they find oil, they move a **production platform** to the place. The crew on the production platform drill wells to reach the oil. Some wells are over three kilometres deep. It can take many weeks to drill through the rock.

Production platform

A production platform is made of steel or concrete. It must be attached firmly to the sea bed. The platform is very big. About 200 people work on a platform. There are the drilling team, engineers, divers, radio operators, cooks and cleaners. People have to live on the platform. They cannot go home at night. They work for about two weeks. Then, they go ashore for two weeks. Work goes on day and night. Everyone has 12 hours' work, then 12 hours' rest. They work hard and earn a lot of money.

◀ Most people travel to and from the oil platforms by helicopter. The heaviest supplies have to be brought by ship.

Life on an oil rig

On the platform there is a dining room, a games room, a television lounge and a small cinema. Helicopters take people to and from the oil rig.

The North Sea oilfields brought trade and new business to ports like Aberdeen in Scotland. There are oil refineries on the mainland. Oil tankers collect the crude oil from the port. The oil industry provides work for thousands of people in the area. The price of oil can drop. When this happens, some oil rigs may be shut down and people may lose their jobs.

▶ These men are part of a drilling team. They have just attached a new length of pipe to the drill. The team have to work quickly so the drilling can continue.

▼ Oil production platforms are designed to stand up to the worst storms at sea. This one in the North Sea is being attacked by a storm with 180 kph winds.

Saving lives

▼ Some beaches in the world are swept by very large waves. The people on this beach in Australia are protected by a team of lifesavers. They keep a constant watch for swimmers in trouble.

There are disasters at sea every year. Some ships sink in heavy storms. Others hit rocks or other ships. Small boats are blown over by the wind and the crew are swept away. Some of the people in these disasters are drowned, but many more are rescued. The people who rescue them often risk their own lives.

Avoiding disaster

In the past, more ships were wrecked and many sailors were drowned. Today, there are fewer risks. Safety standards are high, and ships have better equipment. Most ships have **radar**, which tells them where other ships are. They also have radios. If a ship is in trouble, the crew can tell other ships. The crew hear storm warnings on their radios. They can sail away from the storm. Lighthouses, lightships, and marker **buoys** warn of rocks and shallow waters.

The rescue services on the shore keep a constant watch. The **coastguards** and lifesavers watch out for swimmers in trouble. Rescue boats patrol near crowded beaches. They are ready to rescue swimmers, sailors or windsurfers who need help. Sometimes helicopter crews keep watch from the sky.

Saving lives

To the rescue

The crew of a ship radios for help when a ship is in trouble. The same signals are used all over the world. They are 'Mayday' and 'S.O.S.', which is short for 'save our souls'. Nearer the coast, people in trouble send rockets or flares into the sky. Other boats go to the rescue if they are close enough. The coastguard decides to send a rescue boat or a helicopter. A helicopter is often faster. The helicopter crew can pick up some injured people and take them to hospital. A rescue boat can go alongside and help more people.

In Britain, the Lifeboat Service has rescue boats all round the coast. The crew rush to the lifeboat when there is an alarm. The lifeboats have to go out in rough seas. The work is dangerous. The crew have to rescue people in the worst storms. Lifeboat crews are often given medals for their bravery. In the United States, the Coastguard Service patrols the inshore waters. They are always ready to help anyone in trouble at sea.

▲ Rescue boats must be ready for every kind of trouble at sea. The crew are trained to put out fires. They learn how to treat injuries like burns and broken bones.

▶ Helicopter and lifeboat crews save thousands of lives each year. In Britain, the lifeboat crews are volunteers. Some are local fishermen. The people they go to rescue may be their friends and neighbours.

Our need for water

In many parts of the world, people have as much fresh water as they need. Water is stored and then carried to their homes by pipes. People turn on the taps when they want water. They do not think about how it gets there.

In places with little rain, water is very valuable. The centre of Australia is very dry. People who live there try not to waste water. There are few rivers, so people have to dig wells to find water under the ground. Hong Kong has almost no underground water or lakes and rivers. It rains, but storing the rain water is always a problem.

Caring for water

The water which people drink has to be **treated**. It has to be free from **bacteria** which can cause disease. A family home uses about 3000 litres of water each day. A factory may use 100 000 litres of water in one hour. Used water dirties, or **pollutes**, rivers or lakes. It must be cleaned before it flows away.

Sometimes factories pump dirty water straight into the rivers. It costs a lot of money to clean the water first. Chemicals in the dirty water will kill plants and fish. The fresh water supplies from the river will be spoiled.

▼ In London, some of the old docks on the River Thames are no longer used for ships to load and unload their cargoes. This is St Katherine's Dock. New flats and offices have been built here and there is a museum of old ships.

Our need for water

▲ In the future, icebergs could provide fresh water for dry lands. The idea is still only a dream.

The future

The number of people in the world gets larger every year. More water is needed for them. People are always looking for new supplies of fresh water. Governments have to make sure people take care of the rivers and lakes. Some countries have strict laws about cleaning waste water. People try to clean polluted rivers. Scientists keep checks on the water.

People can change deserts into rich, green farmland if they have water. Some hot, dry countries are near the sea. People have found a way to take the salt out of sea water. The water can then be used as drinking water. Farmers can use it to grow food. New villages and farms can be built. It is not an easy or cheap way to make fresh water. Buildings by the sea can use salt water to cool machines. This saves the fresh water.

Some people have good ideas for the future. **Icebergs** are huge blocks of frozen water. People have made plans to tow icebergs from the Antarctic Ocean to the hot, dry lands. There, the ice would melt and provide fresh water.

Glossary

auction: a sale where the goods are sold to the person who will offer the highest price
bacteria: tiny animals that can cause illness
barge: a flat-bottomed boat. Barges carry goods on rivers and canals
bulk goods: large quantities of goods carried by one ship
buoy: a floating marker which shows shipping lanes or warns of danger
canal: a water channel built across land to join two areas of water. Canals are also built to improve the course of a river and drain the land
clipper: a long, narrow sailing ship built for speed. Clippers carried people and goods over long distances in the past
coastguard: someone who is in charge of safety along a length of coastline. The coastguard keeps watch for ships and people in trouble at sea
container: a large metal box for carrying cargo. The boxes are all the same size and shape. They are carried on ships specially built to carry containers and can be unloaded quickly and easily at ports specially built for container ships
crew: the group of people who work together on a plane or ship
crude oil: oil which is still in the same state as it was when it came from the ground
customs: the place where goods and baggage are checked by government officers. These people make sure that the correct taxes are paid on goods entering or leaving the country. They also check that no forbidden goods are being carried
dam: a strong wall built to hold back a river. A dam is usually built of concrete and is large enough for a lake to be made behind it
delta: a fan-shaped area of land made by the mud, sand and stones dropped by a river at its mouth. The river divides into many channels as it flows through the delta to the sea
derrick: a tower which is made of steel girders. Derricks are built over oil wells or rigs. They support the heavy drilling equipment
design: the way something is made or built and how it looks
dhow: an Arab boat with one large three sided sail
dike: a drainage ditch. Also a long, thick, earth wall built to hold back water and control floods

dock: a place by or on a river, lake or sea where ships can stop to load and unload
draught: the depth of water a ship needs to float in
dredge: to scoop or suck up mud from the bed of a river to make a deep channel for ships
dry dock: a place by or in a river where a ship is repaired or painted. The ship sails into the dry dock and the water is pumped out. The ship rests on blocks while it is worked on. Then, the dock is filled with water again and the ship sails out
dugout: a boat made by hollowing out a tree trunk
economy: the working of a country's money, trade and industry. A government must try to control the economy so that the country does not spend more than it earns
electricity: a type of power
erosion: the wearing away of land by water, ice or the weather
exploration rig: an oil drilling rig which is used to search for oil. Exploration rigs can be moved easily from place to place
export: to send goods to another country to be sold
factory: a building where goods are made by machine
fertile: describes rich soil where seeds and plants can grow well
fishmonger: a person whose business is to sell fish
fitting out: the supplying and equipping of a ship after it has been launched
flood plain: the flat area on either side of a river, over which it floods
fresh water: water that does not contain salt
geologist: someone who studies the rocks and history of the Earth
gut: to remove the inner parts of a fish which are not eaten
harbour: a place where ships can shelter from the open sea
hull: the main body or shell of a ship
hydro-electricity: electricity which has been made by using fast-flowing water to drive a turbine
iceberg: a large quantity of ice which floats in the sea
import: to bring in goods into a country from another country
industry: the work to do with the making or producing of goods
invent: to make something new
irrigation: watering the land by using a system of pipes and ditches. The water is pumped from rivers, lakes, or from under the ground. Crops can grow on irrigated land

Glossary

ivory: a hard, white, bone-like substance which forms the long pointed teeth of elephants, walruses and narwhals

lock: a part of a river or canal with gates at each end. The level of the water can be changed to let ships go 'uphill' or 'downhill'

market price: the price which buyers will pay for something

merchant: a person who buys and sells goods, often with other countries

monsoon: a strong wind that changes direction according to the season

navigation instrument: any instrument which is used to find the way from one place to another

over-fish: to catch too many fish from one place. Over-fishing can make some types of fish die out

pilot: a person who goes on board and steers a ship. A pilot is used when a ship is going in or out of a port, or when it is sailing through dangerous water

polder: an area of low-lying land which was once covered by sea. The land is kept dry by draining it and by the building of earth walls

pollute: to spoil something. When oil is spilled from a ship, it pollutes the water and can kill fish and birds

population: the total number of people living in a country or area of the world

port: a place on a river or sea in which ships can shelter or unload and load their cargoes

power station: a large building where electricity is made

product: something which has been made. Some products are grown, others are made in factories

production platform: a large structure which drills for oil under the sea bed. The platform stands on legs which are fixed to the sea bed

pulp: a soft, wet mixture made by mixing a solid substance, like wood, with water

quay: a place where ships can be tied up to load or unload goods

radar: a way of finding the position of an object. Radio waves are sent out. When they meet an object, they bounce back to the radar set

rapid: a part of the river where the water flows very fast over rocks. The water is usually shallow

reed: a water plant with a long stalk

refinery: a place where the raw, crude oil from the ground is made pure. Petrol, diesel oil and other products are made at refineries

refit: to put new equipment into a ship that was built a long time ago

reservoir: a very large tank or lake where water is collected and stored

resort: a place where people go for a holiday

resource: something which can be used to provide people with the things they need

route: the way from one place to another

salt water: the water found in the seas and oceans. Salt water is made up of many different things. The most common substance is salt

shaduf: a type of machine used to lift water from a river in order to water crops

shoal: a large group of fish swimming together

silt: a mixture of sand and mud carried along by a river and then dropped on the river bed

slipway: a sloping track which runs down a river bank to the water. Ships are built and launched on slipways

spice: a sweet smelling or sharp tasting plant. Spices are made from the seeds, flowers, bark or roots of certain plants. Ginger, pepper and cinnamon are spices

stilt: a long pole which acts as a support. Stilts are used to raise a building off the ground

survey: to make tests and collect information about an area of land above or below the sea

tanker: a ship built to carry large amounts of liquids

terminal: a building at a seaport or airport where passengers or goods gather at the beginning or end of a journey

trade: to exchange goods for money or other goods

trawl: to fish with a big net which is pulled along by a fishing boat. A trawl net has a wide opening which is held open so that the fish swim into it. The fish are swept down to the bottom of the net and trapped

trawler: a fishing boat that pulls a net through the water

treat (water): to purify or clean water so it can be used for drinking

turbine: a wheel with many curved blades. It is turned by water or a gas. Turbines drive the machines which make electricity

warehouse: a building in which goods are stored

waterwheel: a wheel which is turned by the power of moving water. The turning wheel is used to drive machines

Index

Aberdeen 41
Africa 6, 9, 11, 17, 19, 23, 33, 34, 35
Amazon River 6
Amsterdam 33
Andes Mountains 6
Antarctic Ocean 45
Arctic Circle 27
Aswan dam 10
Atlantic Ocean 16, 27, 34
auction 31
Australia 4, 5, 34, 44

Barbados 21
barge 12, 16
boat
 ferry 13, 36
 pleasure 12, 13, 20
 power 13, 20
 rowing 12, 13, 38
 sailing 12, 13, 20, 23, 35, 38
 working 8, 9, 12
Bonny River 17
Boston 33
Britain 28, 43

Canada 8
canal 7, 22, 32
canoeing 13
Caribbean Sea 21
Cartier, Jacques 6
Chari River 11
Charles River 33
Chicago 16
China 26, 33, 34
clipper 34
coastguard 42, 43
Coastguard Service 43
Columbus, Christopher 34
Congo River 6
container 33, 36
container ship 36
cranes 36
crude oil 35, 41
cruise ship 36
customs 9, 37

da Gama, Vasco 33
Danube River 9

deep-sea fishing 24, 26, 27, 28, 29
delta 10
de Orellana, Francisco 6
derrick 40
dhow 19, 38
dike 22
dock 17, 36, 37
dry dock 36, 39
dugout canoe 12
Dutch auction 31
Dutch East India Company 34

East Indies 34
echo sounder 24, 28
Egypt 8, 10, 32
electricity 14, 15
England 13, 33, 34
English East India Company 34
Euphrates River 4, 38
Europe 6, 8, 9, 33, 34, 35, 36
exploration rig 40

farming 8, 9, 10, 11, 27, 45
fish farming 25, 27
fishing 4, 8, 9, 10, 11, 18, 23, 24, 25, 26, 27, 28, 29, 30, 31, 33
fish market 31
fishmonger 30
fitting out 39
floating village 23
flood plain 10
France 12, 16
fresh water 4, 44, 45

Ganges River 8, 10, 12
Germany 12
gondola 32
Great Lakes 16, 17
Greece 21

harbour 5, 8, 20, 30, 33, 39
harbour master 37

harbour police 37
heavy goods 12
holiday resort 20, 21
Hong Kong 11, 23, 44
hydro-electricity 15

Iceland 27, 28
Ijaw people 9
India 8, 10, 12, 33, 34
Indian Ocean 19, 21
industry 8, 13, 14, 17, 18, 19, 27, 33, 39, 41
inland port 7, 16, 17
inshore fishing 24, 27, 31
irrigation 10
Italy 25, 32

Japan 26, 27, 34, 36, 39

Kingsley, Mary 6
Kokoto people 11
Korea 39

Lake Chad 11
Laos 8
Lifeboat Service 43
lighthouse 42
lightship 42
Livingstone, David 6
lock 7, 12, 37
Logone River 11
London 33
long line 24

Madagascar 19
Magellan, Ferdinand 34
marker buoy 42
market price 31
Marlow 13
Marne River 16
Mediterranean Sea 32, 33
Mekong River 8
merchant 32, 33, 34
Middle East 4, 35, 38
Mississippi River 8, 12, 17
monsoon wind 19

navigation instrument 28, 39
Netherlands 12, 22
New England 33
New Orleans 12, 17

New York 36
Nigeria 17
Niger River 9
Nile River 8, 10
North America 6, 16, 17
North Sea 28, 41

oil 17, 35, 36, 40, 41
 refinery 17, 33, 41
 rig 40, 41
 tanker 17, 35, 41
over-fishing 24, 27
oyster bed 25

Pacific Ocean 18, 27
palm oil 17
paper making 14
Paris 16
passenger terminal 36
pearl oyster 19
Peru 6
pilot 37
pleasure boat 12, 13
polder 22
port 7, 8, 16, 17, 19, 29, 30, 31, 33, 36, 37
porter 31
Port Harcourt 17
power-boat racing 20
power station 14
production platform 40
pumping station 22

quay 30, 31, 37, 39

radar 42
radio 28, 42
rescue boat 42, 43
rescue service 42
Rhine River 8, 12
river fishing 8, 9, 10, 11
River Thames 13
river transport 12, 13, 17
Romans 32
Rotterdam 12, 36

sailboard 20
sailing ship 35
salt 4, 19, 33, 45
salt water 4, 45
Scotland 41
Seine River 16
Seychelles 21
shaduf 10

shellfish 25
shipbuilding 33, 38, 39
ship repair 39
side trawler 28
slipway 39
South America 6, 23
South East Asia 8, 23
Spain 25, 28
sponge 19
Stanley, Henry 6
stern trawler 28, 29
St Lawrence River 6, 8
St Lawrence Seaway 16
St Louis 17
surfing 20
survey 40
Switzerland 12

terminal 36, 37
Thailand 8
Tigris River 4, 38
tourism 18, 20, 21, 33
trade 5, 6, 8, 9, 13, 17, 19, 20, 33, 34, 41
trade route 32, 33, 34
trade wind 34
trawler 28, 29
trawl net 25, 28
tug 37
turbine 14, 15

United States 8, 17, 33, 34, 35, 36, 43
USSR 26

Venice 32, 33
Very Large Crude Carrier 35

water pollution 44, 45
waterskiing 21
water sports 20, 21
waterwheel 14
West Indies 33
windmill 22
Windsor 13
windsurfing 20, 43

yacht 20
Yokohama 36

Zaire River 6
Zambezi River 6
Zanzibar 19

48